FREUD

BULLET GUIDE

Robert Anderson

Hodder Education, 338 Euston Road, London NW1 3BH

Hodder Education is an Hachette UK company

First published in UK 2011 by Hodder Education

This edition published 2011

Copyright © 2011 Robert Anderson

The moral rights of the author have been asserted

Database right Hodder Education (makers)

Artworks (internal and cover): Peter Lubach
Cover concept design: Two Associates

British Library Cataloguing in Publication Data: a catalogue record for this title is available from the British Library.

10 9 8 7 6 5 4 3 2 1

The publisher has used its best endeavours to ensure that any website addresses referred to in this book are correct and active at the time of going to press. However, the publisher and the author have no responsibility for the websites and can make no guarantee that a site will remain live or that the content will remain relevant, decent or appropriate.

The publisher has made every effort to mark as such all words which it believes to be trademarks. The publisher should also like to make it clear that the presence of a word in the book, whether marked or unmarked, in no way affects its legal status as a trademark.

Every reasonable effort has been made by the publisher to trace the copyright holders of material in this book. Any errors or omissions should be notified in writing to the publisher, who will endeavour to rectify the situation for any reprints and future editions.

Hachette UK's policy is to use papers that are natural, renewable and recyclable products and made from wood grown in sustainable forests. The logging and manufacturing processes are expected to conform to the environmental regulations of the country of origin.

www.hoddereducation.co.uk

Typeset by Stephen Rowling/Springworks

Printed in Spain

To my father, Peter, who reads all my manuscripts
with equal amounts of indulgence and care

About the author

Robert Anderson is a freelance teacher, writer, editor and translator. He studied Modern Languages at the University of Exeter and went on to live in France for a number of years.

He has taught in schools in France and the United Kingdom and has worked in educational publishing for more than a decade. He has published a wide variety of children's and adult books, including a series of books on design icons for London's Design Museum as well as online courses for the Tate Gallery.

Acknowledgements

I would like to thank everyone at Hodder – especially Sam Richardson, Helen Rogers and Laura Davis – for their support (and patience!) during the writing of this book. My thanks also to David Porteous, David Price and Peter Lubach, editor, proofreader and illustrator respectively.

Robert Anderson, Scott Cottage, Roxburghshire
May 2011

Contents

Introduction

Born over 150 years ago, **Sigmund Freud** continues to loom large in the contemporary world. No other **psychologist** – with the possible exception of his near contemporary Carl Jung – has achieved quite his degree of fame or indeed notoriety. Freudian terms are on everyone's lips, and his ideas – at least in shorthand form – have become commonplace. We talk, for example, about being **in denial**, about having made a **Freudian slip**, and so on…

Freud is best known, of course, for his ideas about **sex** – even for the idea that just about **everything** is about sex – and in this way he is sometimes seen as a kind of **prophet** of today's hypersexualized Western society. Freud was certainly one of many late nineteenth-century thinkers who began to study human sexuality **systematically** and **scientifically**. Nonetheless, his understanding of sexuality was rather different from, or more **complex** than, what it is generally taken to mean today: for Freud it was not so much a brute **animal** instinct than a deeply **human** energy that underpinned the personality in all its diverse aspects.

This brief book sets out to give an **overview** of Freud's thinking and to show how his ideas continue to offer illuminating, stimulating insights into human psychology and behaviour. In recent years Freud's **reputation** as a great and **useful** thinker has taken a bit of a tumble – unfairly, in my opinion. Here I would like to stress his role as an outstanding and courageous pioneer whose **groundbreaking ideas** opened a window onto a hidden, intricate world that had previously been rarely acknowledged, let alone explored.

No other psychologist – with the possible exception of his near contemporary Carl Jung – has achieved quite his degree of fame or indeed notoriety

1 Life and times

The pioneer of psychoanalysis

Freud's **psychoanalytic** theories developed in a particular time and place as well as being the product of a particular, even unusual, personality.

Most of his long life was spent in **Vienna**, which at the end of the nineteenth century was the centre of a thriving medical as well as more general culture. It was in this cosmopolitan city that Freud developed a successful neurological practice and from 1900 began to attract a large number of followers.

**Freud's psychoanalytic theories...
the product of a particular,
even unusual, personality**

Key term: psyche
The term *psyche* derives from the Greek word for 'soul' or 'mind' – the non-physical part of the individual. Freud first coined the word *psychoanalysis* (literally 'analysis of the mind') in 1894, although he had used variants somewhat earlier.

In this chapter we will look at:

* an overview of the **key events** in Freud's life
* Viennese culture at the turn of the twentieth century
* Freud's **personality**
* psychiatry before Freud.

Life

1855	Born 6 May into a German Jewish merchant family in Freiberg (Příbor), Moravia, then part of the Austrian empire and now in the Czech Republic
1860	The Freud family moves to the Austrian capital, Vienna
1881	Becomes a doctor of medicine
1886	Sets up private neurology practice; marries Martha Bernays, granddaughter of Hamburg's chief rabbi
1894	First uses the term psychoanalysis

Key term: neurology
Neurology is the branch of medicine dealing with disorders of the nervous system.

1897	Abandons the 'seduction theory' as origin of hysteria
1906	Begins friendship with the Swiss psychiatrist Carl Jung
1913	Break with Jung
1938	Freud, his wife and daughter Anna flee the Nazis and settle in Hampstead, London
1939	Freud dies 23 September

Key works
1895 *Studies on Hysteria* (with Josef Breuer)
1899 *The Interpretation of Dreams*
1901 *The Psychopathology of Everyday Life*
1905 *Three Essays on the Theory of Sexuality*
1923 *The Ego and the Id*
1930 *Civilization and Its Discontents*

Vienna

From the end of the nineteenth century until the eve of World War I (1914–18), Vienna was the hub of **a vibrant, cosmopolitan culture**. Freud kept himself largely to the professional medical circles to which he belonged. Nonetheless, his thought both reflected and enriched the **broader intellectual currents** dominant in the Austrian capital.

Some of the key cultural figures include (together with representative works):

* the **erotically charged art** of Gustav Klimt – *The Kiss* (1907–8) – and Egon Schiele – *Self-portrait with Physalis* (1912)
* the atonal, **'expressionist'** music of Arnold Schönberg – e.g. String Quartet No. 2 (1908)
* the **sexually frank** plays of Arthur Schnitzler – e.g. *La Ronde* (1900).

It is not especially or necessarily a question of influence here, but of the liberal, open-minded culture of which Freud was a part.

CASE STUDY: Gustav Klimt

Like Freud, Gustav Klimt (1862–1918) was a pioneer whose radical innovations both shocked and fascinated Viennese society. Klimt's daring, gorgeous paintings dealt with some very similar themes to those written about by Freud, including **female sexuality** and the human life cycle of **birth, love and death**.

We cannot be sure that Freud and Klimt ever met, but it seems likely given that they shared common friends (notably Schnitzler). Moreover, the painter's portrait sitters were drawn from much the same (largely female) upper middle-class clientele as Freud's patients.

One of the elaborate murals Klimt painted for the University of Vienna (1903; destroyed) has even been interpreted as reflecting Freud's theory about castration anxiety.

Personality

Freud's personality was **a key ingredient** in the development of his psychoanalytic ideas. During the late 1890s he undertook a sustained period of self-analysis, examining his own dreams, memories, fantasies and fears. He uncovered a violent hostility towards his father and a childhood sexual attraction to his mother.

> ## 'A certain degree of neurosis is of inestimable value as a drive, especially to a psychologist.'
> Sigmund Freud

Freud, though usually warm and tender towards his wife and children, could be difficult and overbearing. His **relationship with Jung**, in particular, showed his capacity for being controlling and dogmatic.

Freud and Jung

Freud thought of the Swiss psychiatrist Carl Jung, who was almost 20 years younger, as his **successor** as the leader of the psychoanalytic movement. In one letter Freud called him his 'crown prince' while Jung spoke of their relationship as like **'father and son'**. In 1910 Jung became the first president of the International Psychoanalytical Association.

Soon after, however, the relationship began to sour. Jung grew impatient with what he considered to be Freud's stranglehold on psychoanalysis, while Freud became increasingly enraged by Jung's new ideas and implicit criticisms of his own (especially his emphasis on the **sexual nature** of the libido). In 1913 the two men acrimoniously split and Jung left the psychoanalytic movement.

Psychiatry before Freud

During the nineteenth century, doctors across Europe increasingly became engaged in the study and treatment of mental disorders – **psychiatry**. At this time large numbers of asylums (psychiatric hospitals) were set up and increasing numbers of people were interned within them.

The predominant model of mental illness developed through the nineteenth century was **neurological** – i.e. illness was considered to be the result of physical disorders of the central nervous system – and the corresponding treatments, too, were primarily biological/medical.

In the 1890s Freud, who trained as a neurologist, originated theories based on the idea that at least some disorders were caused by hidden traumas sustained during patients' childhood development and pioneered a one-to-one speech-based treatment he called **psychoanalysis**.

Jean-Martin Charcot

In 1885 Freud went to study under the French neurologist Jean-Martin Charcot (1825–93) at the Pitié-Salpêtrière Hospital in Paris. One of Charcot's main research areas was **hysteria** – which in the nineteenth century was considered a specifically female illness and was used to describe a broad array of physical symptoms such as nervousness and convulsions.

Charcot believed that hysteria was a **hereditary illness** and could be treated with **hypnosis**. Freud came to disagree with Charcot's understanding of hysteria, which he argued was psychological in origin. Nonetheless Charcot's use of **meticulous observation** as a way of diagnosing his patients' conditions deeply influenced Freud's own thought and practice.

2 The unconscious

Hidden motivations

What makes us act, feel and think the way we do? Sometimes our motivation is obvious: we go to the shops to buy a pair of shoes because an old pair has worn out. But what if we felt *compelled* to buy new shoes every week, regardless of whether we needed them? Our motivation, in this instance, might seem puzzling – even to ourselves.

To explain such hidden motivations, Freud developed the idea of the unconscious.

Note!
In popular usage you often hear the word 'subconscious' to mean 'unconscious', though this is incorrect. Freud's original German term is *das Unbewusste*.

What makes us act, feel and think the way we do?

The unconscious lies at the heart of Freud's thought and psychoanalytic practice. In this chapter we will look at:

* when and how Freud developed the idea of the unconscious
* the key concepts of **id**, **ego** and **superego**
* the **Pleasure Principle** and **Reality Principle**
* how the unconscious affects our everyday lives.

As you read through this chapter, think about whether Freud's view of human nature is positive or negative.

Freud's 'plan' of the psyche

'I set myself the task of bringing to light what human beings keep hidden within them...'

Sigmund Freud

Freud was by no means the first thinker to come up with the idea of the unconscious mind. For example:

* the ancient Indian holy texts known as the Vedas refer to stages of consciousness, including an inner, 'unconscious' world of visions and dreams
* Shakespeare in plays such as *Hamlet* (1601) seems to assume unconscious motivations in his characters.

Freud was the first, however, to study the unconscious **systematically** and to show how exploring it could help those suffering from anxiety or mental distress.

Freud gave his first clear account of the unconscious in *The Interpretation of Dreams* (1899). In this book Freud developed a 'map of the mind':

1 the **conscious** – the everyday part of our minds of which we are *aware*
2 the **unconscious** mind – a much bigger part of our mind full of fears and desires of which we are *unaware*
3 the **preconscious** mind – where unconscious fears and desires are much 'closer to the surface' but of which we are *as yet* unaware.

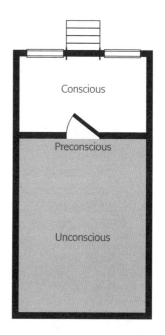

Conscious

Preconscious

Unconscious

● Freud imagined the mind as a house and its different parts as rooms. This idea was an ancient one.

Ego, id and superego

Later, Freud developed a related but slightly different model of the mind. This, too, consisted of three parts:

1 the **ego**
2 the **id**
3 the **superego**.

* The **ego** (the 'I') is characterized by common sense and reason. It struggles to keep control of the id.
* The **id** (the 'it') is made up of the unconscious desires that constantly struggle to express themselves.
* The **superego** (the 'above I') is our conscience – the part of our mind that makes us feel guilty about our desires, whether we are aware of them or not.

18

The job of the ego is to mediate between the conflicting demands of the id and superego.

'One might compare the relation of the ego to the id with that between a rider and his horse. The horse provides the locomotor energy, and the rider has the prerogative of determining the goal and of guiding the movements of his powerful mount towards it. But all too often... the rider is obliged to guide his horse in the direction in which it itself wants to go.'

Sigmund Freud, *New Introductory Lectures on Psychoanalysis*, 1932

The Pleasure and Reality principles

The ego and the id operate according to two opposing principles:

1 The id is always trying to gratify its needs – and without delay! This is the **Pleasure Principle**.
2 The ego realizes that immediate, uncontrolled gratification can cause painful feelings of guilt or even actual harm to ourselves or others. For this reason, the ego learns to defer and/or to moderate its pleasures. This is the **Reality Principle**.

20

Gimme that cake... now!

I'll just have a sliver for now. I have to think of my waistline!

Robert Louis Stevenson

The writer Robert Louis Stevenson (1850–94) did not know about Freud's ideas. Nonetheless, his portrayal of a 'split personality' in *The Strange Case of Dr Jekyll and Mr Hyde* (1886) could be seen as a **powerful depiction** of the Pleasure and Reality principles:

* Dr Jekyll is a sociable, upstanding citizen – a gentleman
* his 'other' self, Mr Hyde, gives free rein to his instincts in all their savagery.

How the unconscious affects us

As evidence for the existence of the unconscious, Freud pointed to three phenomena:

1 As we sleep, our unconscious fears and desires are able to express themselves more freely in our **dreams**.

Key term: neurosis

According to Freud, neuroses are relatively mild **mental disorders** arising in childhood that express themselves in a range of symptoms, most notably **anxiety**. **Psychosis**, by contrast, referred to a much more serious disorder resulting in the sufferer losing contact with reality. The distinction is no longer officially recognized by modern psychiatrists.

2   A maladjusted (too **repressed**) unconscious reveals itself in
    neuroses that can inhibit us from living a full, happy life.
3   Insights into repressed thoughts and desires are unwillingly revealed
    by parapraxes, so-called 'Freudian slips'.

CASE STUDY: Parapraxis

Freud was deeply fascinated by the subject of parapraxis and in
the *Psychopathology of Everyday Life* (1901) he devoted a whole
chapter to a single example. Often his 'explanations' are very long
and involve a complex chain of word associations and buried
memories. In this example, from the fact that a friend appeared to
have forgotten a word from a Latin quotation, Freud deduced that
he was repressing his fear that his mistress was pregnant.

3 Psychosexual development

Sex and sexuality

Freud is often criticized for having 'reduced' everything about human beings to sex. His understanding of human sexuality, however, was rather different and richer than such a caricature would suggest.

For Freud, the sex drive or **libido** was about much more than a simple animal instinct – the helpless, single-minded desire to mate and reproduce. Unlike animals, he argued, human beings have sex lives that exist beyond, and even without, what might be considered conventional sex acts.

At the core of [Freud's] thought was the idea that sexuality influences and shapes our lives from our earliest moments

At the core of his thought was the idea that sexuality – in this broad, rich sense – influences and shapes our lives from our earliest moments.

In this chapter we will look at:

* Freud's understanding of the libido
* homosexuality and fetishism as evidence of the nature of human sexuality
* childhood sexuality and **psychosexual development**
* the role the libido plays in the development of **neuroses**.

As you read through this chapter, think about whether Freud overplayed the role of sexuality in human psychology.

Are there other 'drives' that might be similarly powerful?

The libido

As we saw in the previous chapter, Freud believed that there is an unconscious part of the mind – the **id** – that teems with chaotic, powerful drives. The **libido** is the 'sex drive', an aggressive, amoral energy or force that strives to find pleasure in many areas of human activity, including but not confined to sex.

For Freud, human sexuality was thus not just about 'normal' sex acts, but was deeply wrapped up with human **creativity** and **imagination**.

● 'Do you think she does that as some kind of displacement activity?'

28

Key term: libido

The word *libido* is nothing more than the Latin word for 'desire'. Freud would also later use the term *eros* – after the Greek god of love.

It was Freud's understanding of the libido as primarily sexual that proved to be the vital stumbling block for his follower **Carl Jung** (see Chapter 1). Jung believed that the libido was a much more general 'life energy' that expressed itself across all aspects of human activity.

This may sound like hair-splitting but it opened up a **schism** in the psychoanalytic movement.

Homosexuality and fetishism

Freud argued that the **diversity** and **variety** of human sexuality is suggested by the existence of homosexuality and fetishism. Both of these phenomena show that sexuality is not just about the goal of human reproduction:

* **Homosexuality** – If sexuality were just about 'animal' reproduction, the individual would automatically choose someone – a **sex object** – of the opposite sex.
* **Fetishism** – This shows how the sex object may not even be a person at all, but a thing – a shoe, clothing and so on – and something that may be (though not necessarily) completely divorced from the core sex act (penile-vaginal intercourse). Fetishism also shows the importance of the **imagination** and **fantasy** in human sexuality.

30

Freud and bisexuality

For Freud the libido was naturally free-flowing and could attach itself to any object and either sex. Young children, before the onslaught of the Oedipus complex (see Chapter 4), were **polymorphously perverse**. (*Polymorphous* means 'taking multiple forms'.)

Following the arguments of the Austro-German sexologist **Richard von Krafft-Ebing** (1840–1902), Freud believed that 'all human beings are bisexual and that their libido is distributed between objects of both sexes, either in a manifest or latent form'.

Most people, however, repressed their 'natural' bisexuality throughout their lives, instead adopting a **monosexual** identity – either heterosexual or homosexual.

Childhood sexuality

Freud's most influential idea was that our sex lives begin at birth. This idea was the focus of his 1905 book *Three Essays on the Theory of Sexuality*, in which he set out a model of **psychosexual development** – a series of stages during which the libido is focused on a particular body part, or **erogenous zone**.

During each phase the child finds erotic pleasure in these zones:

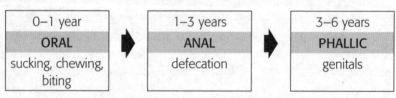

0–1 year	1–3 years	3–6 years
ORAL	**ANAL**	**PHALLIC**
sucking, chewing, biting	defecation	genitals

After the phallic stage comes a period of **latency**, when the libido is in relative abeyance. This lasts until puberty (the **genital phase**), when the individual sexually matures and the libido is 'normally' directed towards an 'appropriate' sexual object – the sexual partner – and 'appropriate' sexual acts (intercourse).

The latency stage

For Freud the latency stage – between roughly the age of six and puberty – is a period of relative calm in a child's psychosexual development and for this reason he pays it scant attention in his writings. Subsequent psychoanalysts have argued that it can, by contrast, be quite a troubled period in the **ego development** of the individual. This is the time when children begin to compare themselves with their peers and may develop **self-esteem** issues.

Fixation and regression

* Sometimes a child may fail to entirely 'move on' from a particular stage, perhaps because the child is punished for 'inappropriate' behaviour or is thwarted in some other way.
* As a consequence, the individual remains emotionally preoccupied – **fixated** – with this stage. In adulthood, at times of stress, he or she will return – **regress** – to the fixation as a way of gaining comfort.
* Fixations may be relatively mild (e.g. thumb-sucking) or occasionally take the form of a serious disorder (e.g. anorexia).

34

'The mind is like an iceberg, it floats with one-seventh of its bulk above water.'

Sigmund Freud

CASE STUDY: Oral fixation

Freud argued that children who are either overfed or underfed during their first year of life may consequently suffer from an oral fixation in adulthood. Typical examples of oral fixation include:

* smoking
* overeating
* alcoholism
* nail-biting
* oral sexual practices
  (fellatio, cunnilingus, etc.)
* even talking too much!

● One form of oral fixation.

4 The Oedipus complex

A family afffair

For Freud, the **Oedipus complex** was the **key psychosexual crisis of childhood**, one whose results had an enormous influence over the rest of the individual's psychological life.

Freud thought of this childhood crisis as a kind of **hidden family drama**, brimming with powerful, disturbing emotions and painful conflicts. Few people, he believed, got through this crisis entirely unscathed.

Perhaps because it was so central to his ideas, the Oedipus complex has attracted a great deal of comment and criticism.

For Freud, the Oedipus complex was the key psychosexual crisis of childhood

In this chapter we will look at:

* **Freud's understanding** of the Oedipus complex
* how the child resolves the Oedipus complex
* **common criticisms** of the Oedipus complex.

● According to Freud, how we negotiate the Oedipus complex during childhood helps shape our adult relationships.

The beginning of the Oedipus complex I

The Oedipus complex begins towards the end of the **phallic stage**, when children begin to notice the anatomical differences between the sexes. The hidden psychic 'drama' that this discovery unleashes differs for boys and girls and becomes associated with their ongoing struggle for independence and autonomy.

Who was Oedipus?

Freud named his complex after Oedipus, the son of Laius, king of Thebes. He was abandoned as a baby but later returned to Thebes where he unknowingly killed his father and then married his mother, Jocasta. When he discovered the truth, he blinded himself.

The boy

1 The boy needs to break free from his mother, who has hitherto seemed all-powerful and whom he **both loves and fears**.
2 The boy identifies with the father, who like him has a penis (**phallus**).
3 This identification gives the boy a sense of his masculine **power**.
4 He still loves his mother, but now this love becomes eroticized.
5 The boy's father is now also a rival whom he **both loves and fears** and whom he also desires to replace/kill.

The parents

Throughout this drama, the parents are not passive 'players'. For example, the mother is to some degree erotically attached to her son, and the father may feel he is in a power struggle with another, younger male. These buried emotions intensify the crisis for the child and help determine how successfully he resolves it.

The boy's father is now also a rival whom he both loves and fears

The beginning of the Oedipus complex II

The development of the Oedipus complex in girls is rather different –
Freud sometimes named it the **'negative Oedipus complex'**.

The girl

1 The girl needs to defend her ego against her mother, who has
  hitherto seemed all-powerful and whom she **both loves and fears**.
2 She cannot identify with her father, who unlike her has a penis.
3 Instead, to win her father's power, she must become his lover.
4 The girl's mother is now also a rival whom she **both loves and fears**
  and whom she desires to replace/kill.

For Freud, the feminine Oedipus complex could be even more
emotionally intense and disruptive than its masculine counterpart,
leaving the adult woman emotionally uncertain and **submissive** and
trapped in an ongoing power struggle with her mother.

42

The Electra complex

The feminine version of the Oedipus complex is sometimes known as the Electra complex, after the daughter of Agamemnon in Greek mythology who revenges her father's murder by helping to murder her mother, Clytemnestra. The term was coined by Carl Jung in 1913, although Freud himself disliked it.

● 'Poor Electra! I think it was more than just a bad-hair day!'

Resolving the Oedipus complex I

As you can see, there are lots of powerful emotions going on in the Oedipus complex…

* love
* fear
* desire for power

…and so on – all of which compete with one another in the child's relationships with its parents. To this potent brew is added the **guilt** the child feels because of its incestuous desire for one parent and murderous feelings for the other!

● The Oedipal boy is swamped by his emotions.

Normally the crisis is finally resolved during puberty (the **genital phase**), when the child learns to overcome these complex feelings and redirect his or her libido towards an appropriate sexual partner. In Freud's view, a successful resolution of the Oedipus complex meant the establishment of a **stable heterosexual relationship**.

Castration anxiety

According to Freud, during the phallic stage boys also develop a castration anxiety. Noticing that girls do not have a penis, boys believe that they have been castrated as a way of punishing them for their 'bad' desires and consequently live in dread of the same thing happening to them. Males, Freud thought, often retain a lingering castration anxiety throughout life, perhaps shown in a fear of powerful or sexually dominant women.

Resolving the Oedipus complex II

Few people, Freud believed, are completely successful in negotiating the emotional turmoil of the Oedipus complex. Even well-adjusted individuals continue to have **'relationship problems'**, not only with their parents but with sexual partners, that reflect residual tensions from this key crisis.

For Freud, however, there were a few more obviously unsuccessful outcomes. For example, *in his view* the **male homosexual**:

* has abandoned his rivalry with his father
* has over-identified with his mother *and*
* has made men – and the phallus – the object of his desire.

This understanding of homosexuality as a kind of failure to 'pass the test' of the Oedipus complex has, understandably, attracted a lot of criticism.

46

CASE STUDY: Little Hans

Freud's study of 'Little Hans' (1909) showed the possibility for **trauma** associated with the Oedipus complex even during childhood:

* Freud conducted his analysis of Little Hans largely indirectly, through the boy's father who was also a psychoanalyst.
* The five-year-old Little Hans suffered from an extreme **fear of horses**, which Freud interpreted as evidence that he was in the grip of the Oedipus complex.
* The fear of horses – known for being well endowed – was in reality a fear of his father, whom he believed would punish him for his sexual attraction to his mother.
* Happily, Little Hans's father was able to reassure his son and he went on to have a normal adolescence.

5 Anxiety and defence mechanisms

Hitting the panic button

Freud was very interested in the troubling emotion known as **anxiety**, whose effects often spill over into the body, causing classic panic symptoms such as rapid breathing and a racing heart.

For Freud, anxiety and the strategies we employ to manage it – the **defence mechanisms** – were a key to unlocking the mysteries of the human mind as well as a useful tool for resolving its hidden traumas.

> **For Freud, anxiety and the strategies we employ to manage it were a key to unlocking the mysteries of the human mind...**
....

In this chapter we will look at:

* Freud's **classification** of anxieties
* his understanding of the original **source of anxiety** in childhood
* his and his daughter Anna Freud's conception of the defence mechanisms.

Are the reasons why we feel panic always obvious?

Types of anxiety

Freud considered there to be **three types of anxiety**:

1 **realistic** – fear of a known threat or challenge in the outside world (e.g. a circling shark, a one-night stand)
2 **moral** – a fear of the tormenting feeling of guilt that can follow on from a 'wrongful' act
3 **neurotic** – an anxiety about something unknown or unexpressed whose origins lie deep in the unconscious.

These kinds of anxiety can overlap. Thus superficial anxieties about having a one-night stand could also hold fears about feeling guilty after the event as well as neuroses about sex itself.

52

Key term: Angst

The German word for anxiety, *Angst* (now often used in English as well), generally refers not to fear of a specific object but to a deep inner **dread** or **malaise**. In the nineteenth century angst was a common theme among writers, thinkers and artists:

* For the Danish philosopher Søren Kierkegaard it was inherent to the human condition – human beings feel anxiety because they **fear responsibility for their lives**.
* Perhaps the most famous visual depiction of angst is the Norwegian painter Edvard Munch's hallucinogenic *The Scream* (1893).

Freud's theory about the **neurotic origins** of anxiety brought a new perspective to the 'tradition'..

The origins of anxiety

Freud saw **anxiety** as being at the **heart of the human condition**:

* We endure unpleasant, 'panicky' feelings of **helplessness** from our birth, when we are forced from the comfort of the womb into the discomfort of the outside world.
* The newborn finds relief from such feelings through its **mother**, who feeds and protects him.
* Later the child feels anxiety of discomfort **in anticipation** of the absence of the mother.
* The child fears the mother because she has the power to **punish** him by withdrawing her protection.
* The child feels **anxiety** about sexual feelings that might provoke the mother's displeasure and therefore represses them.

The trauma of birth and the subsequent anxiety of punishment and loss haunt us throughout our lives.

Do you think Freud's view of anxiety as **inevitable** and as something over which we have **little or no control** is especially helpful?

More recently, for example, some psychologists have argued that we feel anxiety only when we lack the skills to deal with a difficult problem and that such skills can be learned.

'...the act of birth is the first experience of anxiety, and thus the source and prototype of the affect of anxiety.'
Sigmund Freud

Defence mechanisms I

Anxiety can clearly be useful: it can make us act in the face of an impending threat (swim faster in the case of the circling shark) or avoid a situation that will ultimately cause us guilt and pain (the one-night stand).

On the other hand, anxiety can overwhelm us and make life unliveable. One of the key jobs of the ego is to **manage anxiety** so that it remains useful but is not debilitating. Freud called the management strategies adopted by the ego **defence mechanisms**.

● Without defence mechanisms, Freud reasoned, we would be overwhelmed by our anxieties.

Anna Freud and defence mechanisms

Freud's daughter and follower **Anna Freud** (1895–1982) wrote a great deal about defence mechanisms in her important book *Ego and the Mechanisms of Defence* (1936). Drawing on her father's writings as well as on her own clinical practice, she catalogued and explored the numerous ways in which the ego tries to defend itself from anxiety.

Anna Freud also introduced the concept of **signal anxiety** – the important role of anxiety in alerting the psyche to a threat to its equilibrium.

Defence mechanisms II

Key defence mechanisms described by Freud and his daughter include:

* **repression** – the ego banishes to the unconscious feelings that, acknowledged, would cause anxiety (sexual desire, violent anger…)
* **denial** – the ego refuses to recognize or misrecognizes a reality (e.g. someone's death)
* **projection** – a feeling is ascribed to another person rather than acknowledged in the self
* **displacement** – the ego displaces a strong emotion such as anger or aggression onto another, less threatening object
* **sublimation** – unacceptable strong emotions are channelled into a more socially acceptable form (see Chapter 9)
* **regression** – instead of dealing directly with anxiety the ego reverts to a fixated behaviour, such as crying or thumb-sucking, first used during one of the stages of psychosexual development.

Some of these mechanisms are indispensable for our well-being and simply help us get along with our lives. Others (notably denial) are clearly unhealthy. All the defence mechanisms imposed too stringently can become unhealthy: too much repression can lead to neuroses.

As we shall see in the next chapter, overcoming overzealous defence mechanisms can be the key to understanding and 'curing' psychiatric disorders.

All the defence mechanisms imposed too stringently can become unhealthy

● One kind of defence mechanism is refusing to face up to the reality of a situation.

6 On the psychiatrist's couch

A clinical therapy

During the 1890s and beyond, Freud developed **psychoanalysis** in response to his treatment of his mostly female patients (as well as through sustained self-analysis). Psychoanalysis, then, was not just a body of ideas about the mind, but also a **clinical therapy** whose aim was to use these ideas to 'cure' those suffering from psychiatric disorders. Core techniques used during a typical psychoanalytic session included **free association** and **dream analysis**.

Psychoanalysis was not just a body of ideas about the mind, but a clinical therapy

Nonetheless Freud himself admitted that he was much more of a researcher than a therapist, and it was left to his many successors and followers to refine his clinical techniques into more effective treatments.

In this chapter we will look at:

* the key **features** and **techniques** of a 'classical' psychoanalytic session
* some of Freud's **key cases**
* the role of **transference**
* some **criticisms** of clinical psychoanalysis, especially of the psychoanalyst-patient relationship.

The 'talking cure'

Psychoanalysis was early on dubbed the 'talking cure', whose aim was to use a peculiar kind of **two-way conversation** to uncover the repressed causes of psychiatric disorder.

The **classic features** of a psychoanalytic session were established early on:

64

* The patient lies down on a **couch** where he can feel relaxed and comfortable, almost as if he is alone.

● During Freudian psychoanalysis the patient is encouraged to relax as much as possible.

* The psychoanalyst sits away from the patient, hidden from his view.
* The **'50-minute hour'** becomes the standard length of sessions (Freud's sessions were originally very long and gruelling).
* Repeated sessions take place over weeks, months and even years.
* The atmosphere is calm and **non-judgemental**.

The **key techniques** of Freudian psychoanalysis are:

✻ free association
✻ dream analysis (see Chapter 8).

Free association
The technique of free association, which lies at the heart of Freudian psychoanalysis, was developed by Freud's collaborator Joseph Breuer. The psychoanalyst prompts the patient to **relate freely** whatever comes into his mind, wandering from thought to thought and memory to memory. As the patient relaxes, he gradually drops his usual **defences** and reaches thoughts and memories that are usually hidden from him.

Analyst and analysand

* The role of the Freudian psychoanalyst is **to listen and to guide**, and to use Freudian theories such as the Oedipus complex to construct the hidden structures and 'narratives' in the patient's mind.

* For the patient (the **analysand**), psychoanalysis can be a slow and painful process. Ultimately, however, it can be **cathartic** – a kind of psychic spring cleaning that enables the patient to deal better with buried emotional difficulties.

66

'Psychoanalysis is in essence a cure through love.'

Sigmund Freud, in a letter to Carl Jung

Unequal power relations?

Criticisms of the Freudian psychoanalytic session have often focused on the inequality between the analyst and analysand:

* The analyst, critics argue, takes a **priest-like** or even god-like role: he is quite literally **invisible** and **remote** and interprets the patient's suffering using arcane theories and language.

* Critics also point to the **unequal gender relations** that existed in many of Freud's own cases, in which his patients were more often than not young, compliant women.

Subsequent therapies, such as Jungian psychology and existentialist therapy, have tried to 'correct' what they consider to be the imbalanced therapist-patient relationship found in Freudian analysis by insisting on the warm, supportive **presence** of the analyst and the **key role of the analysand** as he works towards understanding his own problems.

Key cases

Freud wrote in detail about a number of cases, using them as **springboards** for his ideas. To protect the patients' anonymity he gave them pseudonyms, although their identities have subsequently become known, even in their lifetimes.

Key cases include:

CASE STUDY: Anna O

Anna O was the patient of Freud's colleague Josef Breuer during the 1880s but her case inspired Freud's **earliest formulation** of psychoanalytic theories and techniques in 1895. Anna O famously referred to free association as 'chimney sweeping'.

CASE STUDY: Little Hans

In 1909 Freud used the case of Little Hans, who suffered from a phobia about horses, to explore his ideas about **childhood sexuality**, especially the Oedipus complex (see Chapter 4). Freud did not treat Little Hans directly but through the boy's father, a professional colleague.

CASE STUDY: Wolf Man

Wolf Man was a Russian aristocrat who underwent psychoanalysis with Freud for many years. His pseudonym derived from a troubling childhood dream he recalled in which he saw a pack of white wolves sitting in a walnut tree outside his window (see Chapter 8). The case, published in 1918, played a key role in the development of Freud's ideas about **psychosexual development**.

Transference

The case of Anna O early on showed the problem of **transference** in clinical psychoanalysis:

● The relationship between analyst and patient can itself provoke complex emotions.

* During her sessions Anna O became erotically attracted to her psychoanalyst Breuer and even imagined she had become pregnant by him.
* Freud argued that in so doing Anna was redirecting (**transferring**) the repressed desires of her childhood onto her psychoanalyst.
* The transferred emotion could be sexual desire but also fear, anger and indeed any strong emotion.
* Initially Freud considered transference to be a hindrance but quickly realized that in fact it could itself be analysed and used to illuminate a patient's mind.

Countertransference

Freud realized that the problem of transference could also work the other way round: the analyst could also become emotionally entangled with the patient and redirect his own buried feelings onto him or her. He called this **countertransference**. 'Every psychoanalyst… must recognize this countertransference in himself and master it,' he warned.

Transference could itself be analysed and used to illuminate a patient's mind

7 The feminine psyche

'What does a woman want?'

Freud studied the **feminine psyche** throughout his life – most of his patients were women, for example – and yet as a topic female sexuality remains oddly marginal in his work.

His core idea, the Oedipus complex, is viewed first and foremost in relation to male sexuality – he tellingly called its female version 'the *negative* Oedipus complex'.

Female sexuality remains oddly marginal in Freud's work

Towards the end of his career Freud wrote:

The great question that has never been answered, and which I have not yet been able to answer, despite my thirty years of research into the feminine soul, is 'What does a woman want?'

How do we explain this rather blithe declaration of ignorance about female sexuality?

In this chapter we will look at:

* Freud as a **product of his culture**
* the concept of **hysteria**
* **penis envy**
* **feminist criticisms** of Freud's ideas.

The role of women

Nineteenth-century Western culture ordinarily conceived women as:

* essentially **passive** and **sex*less***
* the **objects** of (male) desire, never the **subject**
* dependent and inferior.

In this respect Freud was largely **a product of his times**. His own relationship with his wife, Martha, for example, though very loving, was very conventional, as was his conception of gender roles:

* the sphere of women was **domestic** and **home-bound**, primarily concerned with motherhood
* men were active outside the home; their role as fathers was secondary.

Moreover, men and women's psychological differences were, he believed, directly related to their anatomical ones.

'Women oppose change, receive passively, and add nothing of their own.'
Sigmund Freud

Both Freud's sexism and the sexism of his society are evident in his ideas. The **Oedipus complex**, for instance, is based around the precondition of a nurturing mother and a distant, authoritarian father.

'[Freud's] ideas grew out of society. He mirrored in his theories the belief that women were secondary and were not the norm and didn't quite measure up to the norm.'
Sophie Freud, Freud's granddaughter

Hysteria

Although in many ways his views of women were old-fashioned, Freud was unusual for his time in recognizing that women had **sexual desires** at all. He recognized this very early in his career with his treatment of women suffering from so-called **hysteria**.

A female malady

In the nineteenth century hysteria was a term to describe a disorder suffered by women whose 'catch-all' symptoms might include obsessive behaviour, nervousness and hallucinations.

In the late 1890s Freud's understanding of **the origins of hysteria** underwent a dramatic transformation:

1 In three essays written in 1896 Freud initially argued that hysteria was the result of molestation during childhood – this is the so-called **seduction theory**. Freud based his theory on 18 of his own cases (most of whom were women), but seems to have come to his conclusion even though his patients strenuously denied ever suffering sexual abuse.

2 In 1897 Freud abandoned his theory: most of the stories of childhood molestation his female patients told him were **childhood sexual fantasies**. Part of the reason for this shift was his unwillingness to believe that fathers could commit such crimes or that child abuse could be so prevalent as his own cases would suggest.

His abandonment of the seduction theory has often drawn criticism. However, it nonetheless marked a **revolutionary shift** in his understanding of **female sexuality**: women were not necessarily the passive victims of male sexuality, but like men had their own active sex lives.

Penis envy

Nonetheless Freud defined female sexuality, it might be argued, in a **negative** way, against the backdrop of his understanding of male sexuality. This is best seen in his concept of **penis envy**, which Freud developed as a refinement of his ideas about psychosexual development:

1 During the phallic phase both girls and boys become preoccupied with the penis, which is associated with **power**.
2 A girl discovers her own lack of a penis and believes she has been **castrated** as a punishment.
3 She wants to get her own penis and tries to 'win' her father's.
4 She develops an **erotic attraction** towards her father.
5 and so on…

Freud defined female sexuality, it might be argued, in a negative way

For Freud, then, a woman's sexual identity is rooted in the trauma of discovering an **absence**.

Womb envy

Freud's understanding of female sexuality drew a great deal of criticism from some of his followers. The German psychoanalyst **Karen Horney** (1885–1952) thought that Freud – a typical male – was obsessed by the penis and countered with the idea that men, in fact, suffered from womb envy – jealousy of women's ability to conceive, bear and nurture children.

Feminist criticisms

Freud's ideas about female sexuality and women more generally have attracted a great deal of feminist criticism, namely:

* his ideas mirror the **prejudices** of his society and have no universal relevance
* his idea of penis envy says less about feminine sexuality than his own **phallic fixation**
* his **abandonment of the 'seduction theory'** amounts to a 'betrayal' of women: he was more ready to accept the existence of a female sex life than a father's molestation of his own children.

Look at the following quotes about Freud by two well-known feminists.

What do you think they are trying to say and do you agree or disagree with their judgements?

82

'Freudian psychology, with its emphasis on freedom from a repressive morality to achieve sexual fulfilment, was part of the ideology of women's emancipation [in the 1920s]... To Freud, even more than to the magazine editor on Madison Avenue today, women were a strange, inferior, less-than-human species.'

Betty Friedan, author of *The Feminine Mystique* (1963)

'Freud is the father of psychoanalysis. It has no mother.'

Germaine Greer, author of *The Female Eunuch* (1970)

8 The interpretation of dreams

What do our dreams reveal about us?

Freud considered his book *The Interpretation of Dreams* (1899) to be his greatest achievement. He continued to revise the book for three decades, adding new details and even whole sections.

For Freud, the systematic interpretation of dreams was **a key tool for the psychoanalyst**, providing illuminating insights into the unconscious and thus contributing to the removal of neuroses.

Today, however, dream interpretation has lost its central place in psychoanalysis. Dreams are today usually regarded as simply too rich, various and idiosyncratic to offer any clear or helpful 'meaning'.

For Freud, the systematic interpretation of dreams was a key tool for the psychoanalyst

In this chapter we will look at:

* Freud's contribution to **dream interpretation**
* his model of how dreams work and their relation to **neuroses**
* his use of **dreams in psychoanalysis**
* **dream symbols.**

● If only dream interpretation were simple.

Leakage from the unconscious

There have been **'dream books'** since ancient times. Dreams were seen as gifts from the gods, offering advice and glimpses into the future, and needed only to be **decoded**.

Freud, by contrast, wanted to place the interpretation of dreams on a **scientific** basis.

* He argued that dreams were a kind of **leakage from the unconscious** and were thus valuable evidence of the otherwise buried desires of the dreamer.
* In children such **'wish-fulfilments'** were often straightforward: a dream about eating cookie-dough ice cream would mean just that.
* Most adult dreams, however, were harder to understand and required a **sensitive exploration** by both dreamer and analyst to unpick them.

88

CASE STUDY: Irma's injection

In the *Interpretation of Dreams* Freud traced the origins of his interest in dreams, as well as his method for their interpretation, to one of his own dreams, which he called 'Irma's injection'. The dream occurred in 1895:

At a party one of his real-life patients, 'Irma', complains about pains in her stomach, throat and nose. Freud examines her and finds 'whitish grey scabs on remarkable curly structures' in her mouth. Puzzled, he calls over two of his medical colleagues, one of whom has prescribed her an inappropriate injection.

Investigation of the dream revealed that Freud felt deeply guilty about not being able to improve Irma's psychological disorder and that the dream was a **wish-fulfilment** of his desire to lay the blame elsewhere.

The 'royal road'

Freud's model of how dreams worked can be summed up as follows:

The **UNCONSCIOUS** is full of buried desires

During the sleep the **SUPEREGO** that normally keeps the desires under wraps is more relaxed

The desires reach the **PRECONSCIOUS**, but because the superego is not entirely inactive, the desire is distorted and disguised as…

The **DREAM**

As you can see, the formation of a dream is similar to the formation of a **neurosis** – dreams, like neuroses, are **symptoms of repressed desires**.

> ## 'The interpretation of dreams is the royal road to a knowledge of the unconscious activities of the mind.'
>
> Sigmund Freud, *The Interpretation of Dreams*

It's worthwhile comparing Freud's understanding of dreams with that of his erstwhile follower and colleague Carl Jung. Both men shared the view that dreams emerge form the unconscious. However:

Which of the two men's views do you think is more 'positive' – Freud's or Jung's?

Dreams are censored by the superego and are hence distortions of the truth.

Dreams lead us to the recovery of past traumas and repressed desires.

Freud

Dreams are straightforward, offering the dreamer the 'unvarnished, natural truth'.

Dreams lead us forwards to our full human nature, towards future psychic health.

Jung

The dream as a tool in psychotherapy

Because dreams and neuroses were so closely related, Freud believed that exploring a patient's dreams could lead towards an understanding of the cause of a neurosis.

However, using dream interpretation in psychoanalysis was a difficult process:

1 The dream needed to be understood in the **context** of the dreamer's life.
2 The dream needed to be interrelated **as a whole**, not decoded symbol by symbol.
3 The dreamer had to play **the principal part** in the interpretation rather than a meaning being imposed by the analyst.

For these reasons, dreams were to be interpreted in conjunction with other psychoanalytic techniques such as **free association**.

CASE STUDY: Wolf Man's dream

One of Freud's patients, to whom he gave the pseudonym 'Wolf Man', recalled having the following traumatic dream at the age of four:

'I dreamed that it was night and I was lying in my bed. Suddenly the window opened... and I was terrified to see that some white wolves were sitting on the big walnut tree in front of the window. There were six or seven of them... In great terror, evidently of being eaten up by the wolves, I screamed and woke up.'

Over the long years of Wolf Man's treatment, Freud patiently used Wolf Man's associations and memories to interpret the dream as evidence of his having witnessed his parents having sex 'doggy style', causing him both terror and arousal.

Dream symbols

In later editions of the *Interpretation of Dreams*, Freud introduced specific interpretations of 'dream symbols'. For example:

1 Long cylindrical objects such as skyscrapers, keys and pipes were symbols of the **phallus**.
2 Hollow or interior spaces such as a cave, keyholes and bowls were symbols of the **vagina**.

Such simplistic imagery has since become a bit of a 'Freudian' joke and fuel for critics who see Freud as obsessed with 'seeing' sex everywhere. Freud's adoption of such dream symbols is all the more surprising because he himself had earlier suggested it was important to avoid such specific decoding.

Dream interpretation in psychoanalysis today

In the early twenty-first century dream interpretation no longer has quite the key place it once had in early Freudian psychoanalysis. Where it *is* used, there has been a shift in *how* it is used. Broadly stated:

* The patient is usually no longer encouraged to 'free-associate' from the dream to discover its **latent content** – such associations are considered to be merely **additional defences** set up against the recovery of the buried trauma. Instead, the dream is interpreted in terms of its **manifest content**.
* These elements are viewed in **the context of the whole session** – the fact that the patient is relating the dream to the analyst means that he is trying to tell the analyst something about their relationship, however indirectly.

9 Society, morality and creativity

The individual and civilization

Freud applied his theories about the unconscious and psychosexual development far beyond the individual's mental life. He also believed they underpinned **the development of society and civilization** and had implications for the interpretation of **religion** and **art**.

Freud's most influential book in this respect is *Civilization and Its Discontents* (1930), in which he argued that the progress of civilization was achieved only at the expense of individual self-renunciation and suffering.

This aspect of Freud's thought, though fascinating, has often attracted criticism since it wanders far into **philosophical speculation**.

Freud argued that the progress of civilization was achieved only at the expense of individual self-renunciation and suffering

In this chapter we will look at Freud's arguments about:

* how morality is **internalized** within the individual
* the **conflict** between individual happiness and societal well-being
* the **'illusion' of religion**
* art as an expression (or **sublimation**) of sexual energies.

Society and morality

Earlier we saw how children's uninhibited, aggressive energies (sexual or otherwise) are gradually 'tamed' during the **Oedipus complex** and how, in the 'normal' run of things, each individual matures as a more or less 'properly' functioning, heterosexual adult.

Freud extended this argument to show how the whole of society might benefit from, or indeed depend on, this process:

* The individual's **anarchic, rebellious energies** are deflected away from inappropriate activities such as abnormal sexual desire or violence.
* Instead this energy is turned inwards and **feeds the superego**, which, as we saw in Chapter 2, acts as a kind of watchperson or censor of the ego.

In this way, Freud says, the moral norms of society are **internalized** within the individual.

Freud's analysis of morality as a **by-product** of the Oedipus complex has been widely criticized:

* It interprets morality as arising solely as the result of **fear of punishment** by the parent – hardly the basis for a healthy psyche.
* It seems to discount the idea that moral behaviour may emerge from a **warm, empathetic relationship** between parent and child.

'The poets and philosophers before me discovered the unconscious; what I discovered was the scientific method by which the unconscious can be studied.'

Sigmund Freud

A happy society, unhappy individuals

Thus, for Freud, repression helps ensure not only:

* the **continuation of heterosexual family life** and the perpetuation of the species, *but also*
* the creation of **an ordered and moral society**.

This is achieved, however, only at great cost: the individual is condemned to live a masochistic life of repression, frustration and neuroses. In short, because they have very different needs and aims, the individual and society are constantly engaged in a kind of **hidden war** with one another.

The individual and society are constantly engaged in a kind of hidden war with one another

Freud's cultural pessimism

The destruction unleashed by World War I led Freud to a somewhat bleak view of the future of mankind. In *Civilization and Its Discontents*, he wrote:

'The fateful question for the human species seems to me to be whether and to what extent people's cultural development will succeed in mastering the disturbance of their communal life by the human instinct of aggression and self-destruction. It may be that in this respect precisely the present time deserves a special interest. Men have gained control over the forces of nature to such an extent that with their help they would have no difficulty in exterminating one another to the last man. They know this, and hence comes a large part of their current unrest, their unhappiness and their mood of anxiety.'

Religion

Although he was born into a Jewish family, Freud was an ardent atheist and indeed **hostile** to religious belief. Nonetheless, he remained fascinated by the psychology of religion throughout his life, writing about it in such books as:

* *Totem and Taboo* (1913)
* *The Future of an Illusion* (1927)
* *Moses and Monotheism* (1938).

104

The soul

Freud used the German term *Seele* ('soul') quite often in his works, although never in its religious or supernatural sense. For him, it referred to an individual's innermost being, their authentic self. For this reason, in English translations *Seele* is often dropped or mistranslated as 'mind'.

For Freud, religion was an **'illusion'**, a wish-fulfilment that emerged from the psyche as it struggled with the Oedipus complex:

1 The child desires the mother and fears the father, who represents authority.
2 The child represses this conflict and instead projects his fear onto an eternal father figure – God.

Religious belief was thus, Freud thought, 'comparable' to **a childhood neurosis**.

Freud's blanket refusal to countenance a **spiritual aspect** to the human psyche aligns him squarely with the zeitgeist ('spirit of the times') of twentieth-century Western society and culture.

Do you agree with this assessment?

'At bottom God is nothing more than an exalted father.'
Sigmund Freud

Sex and art

Freud saw **creativity** as another way in which the individual can deal
with the anarchic sexual energies of the id:

* Most of this energy is **repressed** or otherwise deflected.
* Sometimes, however, the energy can be **expressed** in a socially
  acceptable or useful way – e.g. through creativity. Freud called this
  process **sublimation**.

106

Note!
Today many art historians are suspicious of using
psychoanalytic biography as a key for understanding a
painting, sculpture and so on. They more often prefer to
interpret art works as artefacts **consciously conceived** in a
specific **cultural and social context**.

* For Freud, creativity and neuroses are closely allied, and artistic objects such as paintings and sculptures can be read almost as **neurotic symptoms**, offering insight into the artist's unconscious.

CASE STUDY: Leonardo and the vulture

In 1910 Freud wrote a long essay on the Renaissance artist **Leonardo da Vinci** and his painting *The Virgin and Child with St Anne*. Freud believed that, viewed sideways, the Virgin's cloak took the form of a **vulture** and related this to Leonardo's childhood memory of being attacked by a vulture while in his cradle. Freud argued that Leonardo's memory was in fact a childhood fantasy and related it to his memories of being **suckled** at his mother's breast. While aspects of Freud's argument have today been discredited, the essay offers a fascinating insight into his associative method.

10 After Freud

The influence of Freud

During the early decades of the twentieth century Freud attracted a large number of **followers** among psychiatrists, not only in Vienna but across Europe and America and elsewhere:

* many of these psychiatrists developed their own ideas
* some, like Jung, even broke away from him altogether – a development that hurt Freud deeply.

Freud's ideas were also influential among **modernist artists** and **writers**, for whom his explorations of the unconscious in particular opened up a whole new inner world.

Perhaps in part *because of* Freud's dominant position as the 'father of psychoanalysis', in the second half of the twentieth century his influence – both in psychiatry and the arts – dwindled.

Freud's explorations of the unconscious in particular opened up a whole new inner world

In this chapter we will look at:

* some of Freud's principal psychiatrist followers
* the influence of Freud on **literature**
* the influence of Freud on **art**, especially the Surrealists
* Freud's **reputation** today.

As you read through this chapter, think about why Freud's ideas might have lost some of their power and influence.

Do you think Freud is still a 'great' or 'useful' thinker?

Global influence

Very quickly Freud's ideas influenced other psychiatrists and neurologists around the world:

1902	Freud founded an informal group of like-minded psychiatrists who met in his apartment in Vienna to discuss his ideas and present papers (this later became the **Vienna Psychoanalytic Society** (VPS))
1908	The first **International Psychoanalytic Congress** held in Salzburg, Austria
1910	Freud founded the **International Psychoanalytical Association** (IPA), which helped to spread his ideas around the globe (Jung was appointed the first president)
1911	Foundation of the **American Psychoanalytic Society**
1913	Foundation of the **London Psychoanalytic Society** (in 1919 renamed the British Psychoanalytic Society)

2010	The **centenary of the IPA** celebrated at its congress in Mexico City

Freud's followers

* **Otto Rank (1884–1989)** First president of IPA; spread Freud's ideas in France and the USA.
* **Alfred Adler (1870–1937)** President of VPS; broke with Freud in 1911 to found his own 'school' of psychoanalysis.
* **Carl Jung (1875–1961)** Swiss psychiatrist whose relationship with Freud was initially very close, but who broke from his mentor in 1913.
* **Anna Freud (1895–1982)** Freud's daughter who developed the field of child psychoanalysis.
* **William Reich (1897–1957)** Austro-American psychoanalyst who later in life introduced controversial techniques (such as touch) into psychoanalysis.

The Surrealists

Freud's influence on art is most apparent in Surrealism, which reached its heyday in the late 1920s and 1930s. Prominent members of the movement include:

* Salvador Dalí
* Max Ernst
* Joan Miró.

The impact of Freud is evident in:

* the Surrealists' interest in the **unconscious** and the world of dreams
* their concern with **sexuality**
* their use of spontaneous, **'automatic' art techniques** (e.g. collage, frottage, etc.) which parallel Freud's technique of free association.

CASE STUDY: Salvador Dalí

Dalí first discovered Freud in the early 1920s when he read *The Interpretation of Dreams*. 'It was one of the greatest discoveries of my life,' he wrote. 'I was obsessed by the vice of **self-interpretation** – not just of my dreams but of everything that happened to me, however accidental it might at first seem.' The encounter with Freud had a revolutionary impact on his art, giving him the courage to paint the bizarre and seemingly **disconnected imagery** he found within himself.

Writers and Freud

Many writers, too, took up Freud's ideas and explored human personality and motivation with a new, and sometimes disturbing, depth. Here are two well-known examples:

Virginia Woolf

In books such as *To the Lighthouse* (1927), the English novelist's determination to plunge into the inner life of her characters using her pioneering **'stream of consciousness'** technique shows the influence of Freud. Nonetheless, she was often critical of his ideas, especially of what she perceived to be his sexism.

D. H. Lawrence

In his novels, for example, *Women in Love* (1920), Lawrence explored his characters' **hidden sex lives**. He often used what appears to modern eyes as rather blatant animal symbolism such as rearing horses and frenzied rabbits to suggest powerful, repressed desires.

The Anglo-American poet W. H. Auden was a great admirer of Freud and wrote an elegy on his death in 1939. For Auden, the work of the psychoanalyst and the poet both involved a descent into the 'underworld' of the unconscious to **recover the past**.

Freud today

By the 1970s Freud had been toppled from the central place he once enjoyed both within psychiatry and in academic research more generally. This might be explained by:

* **scientific** criticisms of his concept of the 'layered' mind
* **feminist** criticisms of his view on female sexuality
* **therapeutic** criticisms of the 'oppressive' nature of the Freudian psychoanalyst-patient relationship
* **philosophical** criticisms of his view of the individual as the 'victim' of unconscious drives (thus denying his or her free will).

In the late twentieth century **pharmacological** treatments of mental disorders became dominant in psychiatry.

For all that, Freudian psychoanalysis is still flourishing today:

* the International Psychoanalytical Association has more than **12,000 members** practising in some **30 countries** around the globe

* researchers in the field continue to extend and revise Freud's discoveries
* Freud's writings themselves continue to offer an extraordinarily rich and illuminating treasure trove of insights into the human mind.

> **'Psychoanalysis still represents the most coherent and intellectually satisfying view of the human mind that we have.'**
> Eric Kandel, Nobel Prize-winning neurophysiologist

Freud's writings continue to offer an extraordinarily rich and illuminating treasure trove of insights into the human mind

Further reading

The key here is to read Freud's works themselves, which are available in good, accessible English translations. The works to start with are those from around the beginning of the twentieth century: *The Interpretation of Dreams*, *The Psychopathology of Everyday Life* and *Three Essays on the Theory of Sexuality*. Freud's case studies of, for instance, 'Dora' and 'Little Hans' are also fascinating reads. All these works are available in some excellent Penguin Modern Classics collections of Freud's works, while there is also Peter Gay's massive and good-value compendium *The Freud Reader* (Vintage, 1989). The latter includes Freud's influential though contentious work *Civilization and Its Discontents*.

The following **websites** offer useful information:

* www.ipa.org.uk – website of the International Psychoanalytical Association
* freudfile.org – online resources about Freud
* www.freud.org.uk – website of the London Freud Museum